How to Have More

CONTROL

Over What

Happens

to You

How to Have More CONTROL Over What Happens to You

Selina Jackson, M.A.

gatekeeper press™
Columbus, Ohio

How to Have More Control Over What Happens to You

Published by Gatekeeper Press
2167 Stringtown Rd, Suite 109
Columbus, OH 43123-2989
www.GatekeeperPress.com

Library of Congress Control Number:

ISBN (paperback): 9781662932601

Disclaimer

Acknowledgments

Thanks to all the educators I have worked with over the years who helped spark these ideas. Their experience, feedback, and professional knowledge were invaluable.

Thanks to all the students I have worked with over the years, particularly those who allowed me to try various ideas and explore the many ways to improve student learning and success. Their patience, cooperation, and most of all, sense of humor helped to keep us all among the sane.

Thanks to my family for listening for hours to my "creative genius" in preparation for action, and for loving and encouraging me.

This workbook is dedicated to the memory of Kembleton Wiggins, Ph.D., Ed.D., my friend, colleague, and mentor. You know I could write a book about you, your brilliance, and your support alone. Let it suffice to say I appreciate you, I recognize the gift, and I thank you for continually encouraging me to pursue my dream. Without you, I would never have done it.

Selina Joy Jackson, M.A.

Pre-program Survey

DIRECTIONS: Read each statement carefully. If you agree with the statement, write *True* in the blank. If you disagree, write *No* in the blank.

1. Hitting is the best way to protect myself. _____

2. Other people sometimes make me mad. _____

3. Sometimes at school, I have to be mean to get what I want. _____

4. My anger causes problems for me. _____

5. Good grades are important to me. _____

6. The teachers are responsible for my education. _____

7. Sometimes I have to cuss someone out. _____

8. I expect to be a college student someday. _____

9. I can control how I feel. _____

10. Other people decide what my future will be. _____

11. I worry about my safety in school. _____

12. Before I do anything, I usually think about what could happen. _____

13. If my friend does something bad, I keep it a secret. _____

14. I worry about what others will think if I avoid a fight at school. _____

15. Having fun is more important than learning. _____

16. I can change how I feel by changing how I think. _____

Pre-program Survey, continued

DIRECTIONS: Please answer the questions below in your own words.

1. Is it easy for you to pay attention to the teachers when you're at school? Why or why not?

2. How does your family influence your decisions?

3. What will you be doing one year from now?

4. What will you be doing five years from now?

Table of Contents

1. Rate the quality of your life

2. Find out how to improve the quality of your life

3. Take steps toward a more satisfying life

1. Discover some things that are important to you

2. See how to get out of "baby mode" and get into the action

3. Change your choices to change your life

1. Know the "right" moves for taking charge

2. Use "school behavior" that works for you, not against you

3. How to get better responses from people

Introduction:
How This Book Relates to You

What's up? I'm Selina Joy Jackson, and I wrote this book for you and other young people like you. Why? Because my growing-up years were rough. Really rough.

For example:

- **2 years old –** I was found alone on the kitchen counter trying to cook for myself because I was hungry.

- **5 years old –** A stranger took me, and I escaped.

- **6 years old and 12 years old –** My mother had very difficult times.

- **15 years old –** My mother died, and I went into foster care.

- **16-17 years old –** I bounced around from foster home to foster home.

- **18 years old –** I aged out of foster care. Fortunately, my story doesn't end there.

As you can see, at two years old, I was doing things that a two-year-old should not have to do. By my mid-teens, I was labeled "at-risk." That means some adults expected me to drop out of school, become a drug addict, or worse.

I thought, "Why should this happen to <u>me</u>?" I became very angry about having a difficult life. I felt resentful toward people whose lives looked easier than mine.

If you're angry about having a difficult life, I don't blame you for feeling that way. You have a good reason to be angry, but anger can't do anything to make your life better.

When we have difficult times, we often feel afraid and find reasons to avoid further risks. Then our "reasons" become excuses. Excuses may sound like:

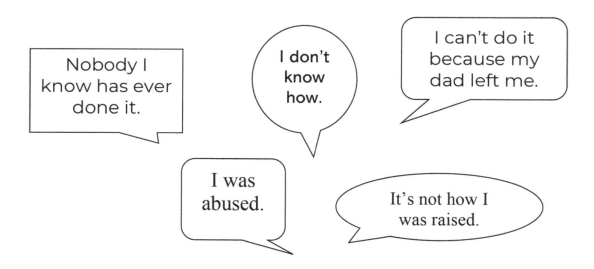

And so on. We give all kinds of reasons why we can't. When we do that, we're "excuse-ing" ourselves from success.

You're not alone, though. I've done that, too.

Complaining is like being in a rocking chair: it feels good, but it gets you nowhere. It is time to get out of the "rocking chair" and change your life.

Here's a heads-up: I'm explaining how to really change your life, so I don't sugar-coat anything or come off softly. I'm bringing the real deal. You can learn something here, put it to good use, and enjoy your better life!

With your extra success and happiness in mind,

Selina Joy Jackson, M.A.

Are You Ready to Learn Something New and Powerful?

This book was written especially for you. If you read it and do ALL the exercises, you will get more control over what happens to you. This means you will feel happier, stronger, and even more positive more of the time. Now, who doesn't want that?

Introducing Our Agents!

You are not here by chance. You are here because you want to be happier and more successful. Certain skills can help you get what you want and avoid needless trouble. Our agents will be on these pages to make it easier and more fun.

This is Agent Motion. He flies around a lot, so that's why he needs that fancy purple cape—and that's also why his hair is rather wild-looking.

If you don't have the skills we show you in this workbook, you'll struggle, you'll miss out on important opportunities, and you could even lose friends and the respect of people around you. Don't miss out on having a much more enjoyable life!

Think of this book as "Gaming for Life Success." You can choose to apply the powerful strategies in this workbook to get more of what you want.

If you complete every page in this book, you'll know how to have a lot more control over what happens to you. That means your life can be better than ever before!

Here's Agent A. She is often quiet,
but people know she's smart,
so they respect her advice.
She likes to be outside, especially
when it's windy.

Agent B seems to just stand around a lot, but he
keeps an eye on what's happening. His quirky
humor causes Agent Motion and Agent A to roll
their eyes a lot.

Chapter 1
THE GOOD LIFE

Chapter Goals:

(Setting goals is the first step to taking control of your life.)

1. Rate your life
2. Find out how to improve your life
3. Take steps to a more satisfying life

It is okay for you to feel exactly how you feel right now because it's a human response, and it will pass.

Agent Motion

A High-Quality Life

- What is a "high-quality life"?
- How do you get the quality of life you deserve?
- Who is in charge of what's happening in your life?

Today:

- **Learn:** Welcome to the School of Hard Knocks
- **Discuss:** Hard knocks
- **Activity:** Quality of Life check-in sheet
- **Wrap-Up:** You don't have to be a victim

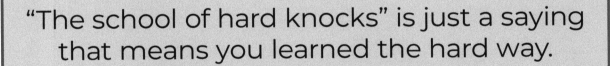

"The school of hard knocks" is just a saying that means you learned the hard way.

We all have a tough story to tell.

What's yours?

Think and share:

1. Walk around the room and find a partner.
2. Listen to your partner's story, then share something that has been difficult for you.

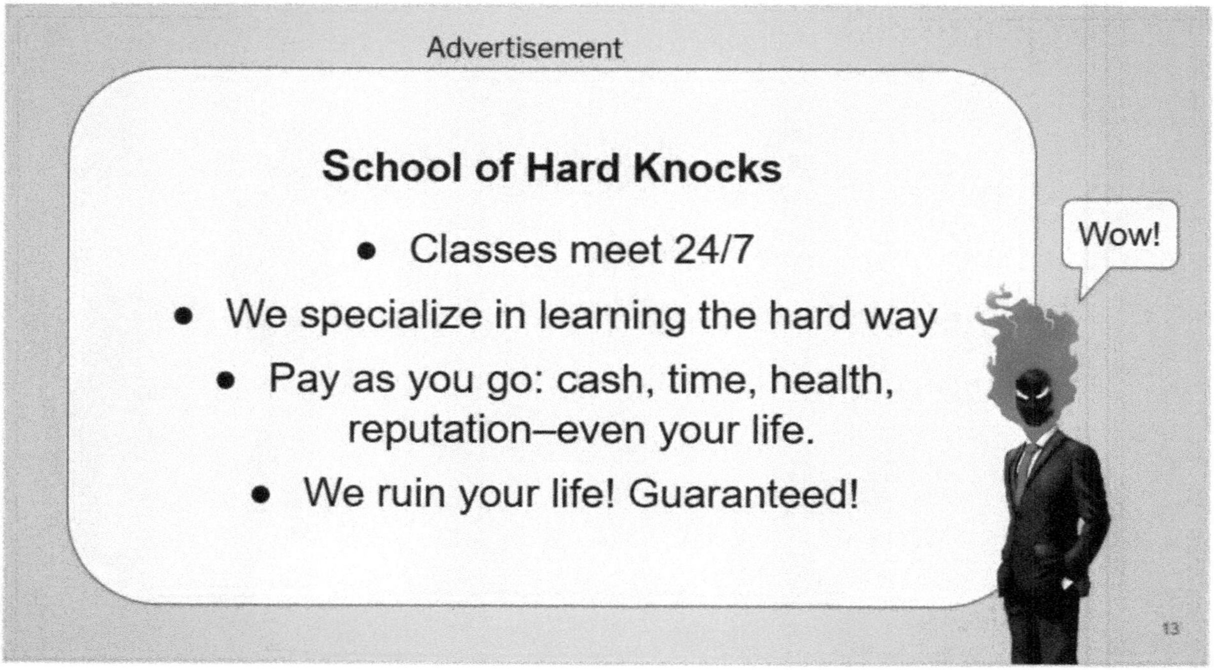

3. What are some things you've learned the hard way?

_____

_____

_____

_____

_____

_____

_____

Ms. Jackson attended the "school of hard knocks." Her growing-up years were not easy, as you saw in the introduction of this workbook.

When you learn the hard way, lessons are available 24/7, but you're likely to fail because the tests are given <u>before</u> you learn, not after. Your lessons are often costly and painful for you, your family, and your friends.

Ms. Jackson said, "Nobody was talking about how to grow up easily and enjoyably, how the mind works, how to get what I needed, or how to avoid preventable problems, so for a long time I got knocked around by situations I had unknowingly created."

What changed?

What changed?

Here's what changed. Ms. Jackson discovered a very valuable idea: Give to Get. To get something, you have

to give something. That's how the world works, so she decided to take control of her situation. She started by giving some of her time to herself— by reading about psychology, education, and many other topics. She learned more about herself and decided what she wanted. She wanted a better life.

Rate the quality of <u>your</u> life. Circle the number that shows where your life is today.

Complete
disaster

Amazingly
wonderful

1   2   3   4   5   6   7   8   9   10

QUALITY OF LIFE
CHECK-IN SHEET

1. Do you feel satisfied with the quality of your life right now? Yes ___ No ___

2. When was the last time your life felt like a "complete disaster"?

   _____

   _____

   _____

3. What was that like?

   _____

   _____

   _____

4. Is that what you really want? Yes___ No___

5. Describe a few times that your life has been "amazingly wonderful." Two examples from Ms. Jackson: I saw A's on my report card, and I made the winning shot in the basketball game.

   _____

   _____

   _____

6. Write a few examples of what you might hear when your life is amazingly wonderful, such as laughter and compliments.

_____

_____

_____

7. Write a few examples of how you feel when your life is amazingly wonderful, such as feeling proud or confident.

_____

_____

8. Write a few steps you could take to make your life amazingly wonderful, starting with things you could do right now.

_____

_____

_____

Agent A on "Quality of Life"

It's important to do all the exercises in this workbook because they show you how to improve the quality of your life. That's a lot better than having to discover all these things by yourself!

Everyone makes mistakes. Do you want to learn from other people's mistakes—or do you want to make all those mistakes yourself?

You'll learn how to figure out what leaders are doing—and you can use that knowledge to accomplish exactly what **you** want to do!

You'll see how top decision-makers target their game and make expert moves. You'll see how to handle the hard facts, choose your response, and move right into the action.

The written exercises train your brain to play an active role in your success.

So, let's get started!

QUALITY OF LIFE
SURVEY

Mark each item true or false.

		True	False
1	You stay out of trouble.		
2	Most of the time, you feel physically strong and healthy.		
3	Your classmates treat you with respect.		
4	You know people you can talk to about almost anything.		
5	You are usually calm.		
6	You have fun safely.		
7	You handle stress in problem-free ways.		
8	Without creating problems, you can get others to smile.		
9	You try to do your best in school.		
10	You can get what you want without creating problems.		
11	You can get adults to say "yes" when they'd usually say "no."		
12	You have a hobby that you enjoy.		
13	In school, you laugh often.		
14	You enjoy your schoolwork.		
15	You have some kind of success most days.		
16	You get along well with your teachers.		
	How many "true" answers do you have?		

Guess what? You can find your score on the next two pages.

QUALITY OF LIFE
SURVEY RESULTS

Leader, Decision-maker *(You get things done)*

15-16 "True" answers.

✓ You use the "give to get" strategy.

✓ You do things now that will pay off later.

✓ You know money and "the good life" come with education, so you're earning good grades.

✓ You are strong, in charge, and a master of the game.

Jr. Executive *(Keep movin' up!)*

13-14 "True" answers.

✓ You usually use the "give to get" strategy.

✓ You usually do things now that will pay off later.

✓ You see money and "the good life" come with education. By working smarter (not harder), your grades are improving.

✓ You are getting stronger.

Apprentice *(Learning the trade)*

11-12 "True" answers.

✓ You sometimes use the "give to get" strategy.

✓ You often do things now that will pay off later.

✓ You see some value in education. You know you'll get more good things when you study as the decision-makers do.

✓ Your grades steadily improve as you give more attention to details.

✓ Avoid "bench warmer" status. You could be in the game!

Unemployable *(Could be at the "school of hard knocks")*

10 or fewer "True" answers.

✓ You don't use the "give to get" strategy.

✓ You don't do things that will pay off later.

✓ You don't see the value of education—the money and "the good life" it brings.

✓ You don't even realize a game is being played, but in fact, you're the one getting played.

One question: Do you want to wait until things are even worse before you make a change?

If you don't take charge of your life, somebody else will!

Power Play

When talking with your folks, teachers, or other helpful adults, stand at a 90° angle rather than directly face-to-face. This will help them feel like you're both on the same team.

90°

GAMEPLAY

A game to empower you

How to Push Your Own Happy Button

One easy, powerful way to feel happier is to express gratitude.

1. Look for something beautiful.

2. Take a picture of it.

3. Think of someone you care about.

4. Send them a text message with the picture. Tell them what's good and beautiful about the picture and how it reminds you of them. Then, tell them how grateful you are to have them in your life.

5. Choose to give yourself permission to feel good about yourself and what you've done to add to the goodness in our world.

CLASSROOM VIDEO WATCH

Here's a fun exercise that can help you overcome stress!

Video: "Am I Clouding My Own Vision?"

https://www.youtube.com/watch?v=g3BwHoqNl84

...or go to YouTube

and search for EMOMASTERS or SELINAJOYJACKSON.

Whenever something happens that you don't like, you have the power to change how you think about it so you can feel better.

Of course, it's up to you.

What Is Most Important to You?

DIRECTIONS: For each value, check the box that matches how you feel.

Value	Very Important	Important	Somewhat Important	Least Important
Family				
Wealth				
Honesty				
Freedom				
Friendship				
Good health				
Respect				
Adventure				
Knowledge				
Recognition				
Power				
Creativity				
Helping others				
Safety				
Beauty				
Fun				
List 2 more:				

From the list above, which are the five most important values to you?

_____   _____   _____

_____   _____

Applying Your Values Easily

Based on what you value most, which of these careers sound enjoyable to you? Put a checkmark by the ones you might enjoy doing:

___Owning a company that provides security to celebrities

___Designing clothing, shoes, or furniture

___Being the owner of a very successful housecleaning business

___Being a doctor or other health care professional

___Doing what you love to do and getting paid well for it

___Running your own music production company

___Being a sports agent

List two other careers or jobs that you might enjoy:

1. _____

2. _____

Talk to people you know about topics that interest you. Ask questions like, *"I love beauty and friendship; how can I turn that into a successful business?"*

Go online (with your parents'/guardians' permission) and type in one of your most important values listed in the survey. You'd be surprised at how many ideas come up for creating wealth or a great career for yourself. So, what did you discover about yourself?

_____

_____

One or two things you like: _____

_____

_____

One thing you now know about values: _____

_____

_____

One thing that surprised you: _____

_____

_____

Your Goal Achievement Sheet

Answering these questions will 1) help you focus,
and 2) keep you from feeling overwhelmed.

1. What do you want to accomplish in school this year?

_____

_____

_____

2. How will you make that happen?

_____

_____

_____

3. What has stopped you from accomplishing your goals until now?
    What if you decide to let nothing stop you?

_____

_____

_____

Imagine your life as amazingly wonderful. How would it be different from your life today?

_____

_____

_____

_____

What else could you do to make your life amazingly wonderful?

_____

_____

_____

_____

_____

_____

_____

Chapter 2

WHAT DO YOU SEE?

Chapter Goals:

1. Discover some things that are important to you
2. Get out of "Baby Mode" and get into the action
3. Change your choices and change your life

What animal do you see?

Getting Down to It

Have you seen this picture before today? Almost everyone sees one animal right away; then they see the other.

You probably noticed that the rabbit's ears became the duck's beak.

Yes, some things are easier to see when you look at them from a different perspective (position).

Part of growing up is seeing things from a different point of view. That skill can help you get others to say "yes" when they would otherwise say "no."

ARE YOU IN "BABY MODE"?

When we are young and unable to take care of ourselves, we lack experience. We trust those around us to make decisions for us. We trust them with our emotions and our lives because we don't know any better. As time passes, we experience, learn, and grow.

When we're babies, we can't understand everything. When we're very young, we can only understand things from our own point of view. Babies only see things one way—theirs. Are you stuck in baby mode?

EXPRESS YOURSELF

Name three things that are important to you but not important to your folks:

_____

_____

_____

Name three things that are important to your folks that you don't care about very much.

_____

_____

_____

You can see that you and your folks think different things are important. That means you understand that different things are important to different people. You're out of baby mode!

Now you can figure out how to get more control over what happens to you.

The benefits? You will get to choose who you hang out with, and you'll get to choose when and how to enjoy your happiness. Now, who doesn't want that?

How?

How do you get more control over what happens to you?

We'll find out how, but first you need to realize:

- Life has variety. The world has people of all shapes, colors, sizes, ages, and beliefs.

- Different things are important to different people.

- You can decide on a good way to have more control over your life.

- When you have more control over what happens to you, you will have many, many options open up for you.

Looking at things from different perspectives means you ask yourself questions like, *"How could I have done this differently?"* Or *"What is a better way for me to get that?"*

Listen Deeply

You're older now, so you can look at things in a more mature way. You will change your life as you change your choices. Avoid getting stuck doing things one way. Instead, see the unlimited possibilities. Then you get to choose which options to use— and when to use them.

Yup. Fact!

GAMEPLAY

Cell Phone Magic

If you have a cell phone, take a quick selfie. Now, look at the picture for 30 seconds. Resist the urge to delete and retake it. Just look at the picture.

OK. Did you notice your thoughts? Were they helpful? Or were they critical? Did you first notice things you didn't like? Or did you first find the things you like most?

Many people focus on what they DON'T like about their appearance, but that creates stress. What if you decided to focus on good things from now on?

Your Best Friend Is *What Kind of Animal?*

This activity is a fun way to train your brain to start seeing things from different perspectives.

DIRECTIONS: Choose someone to write about:

family member   famous person

friend   teacher   classmate

Write the name of the person you're thinking about:

Now, give your brain a game: imagine this person in some interesting (and FUN) ways. See the next page.

DIRECTIONS: Describe the person you're thinking about:

If this person were a toy, what toy would they be? Why?

_____

_____

If this person were a food, what food would they be? Why?

_____

_____

If this person were a sport, what sport would they be? Why?

_____

_____

What instrument would they be? Why?

What animal would they be? Why?

What car would they be? Why?

I like doing silly things like this!

Congratulations! You've just jump-started your brain to learn to see things from more than one perspective. This will help you get more of what you want while avoiding needless trouble.

The "What If"
Power Flip

(so you can feel better right now)

Examples of negative questions	Examples of positive questions
What if I lose?	What if I win?
What if I fall and people laugh at me?	What if I dance and people are impressed?

Think of a problem you're facing.
Write about it here:

_____

_____

_____

_____

_____

_____

_____

_____

EMOTIONS

frustrated   angry   sad   afraid

happy   relieved   hopeful

excited   worried

...or?

Now it's your turn:

- List three negative "what if" questions about that situation.

_____

_____

_____

How would it feel if your worries came true?

_____

_____

_____

Then, flip each question to make it positive.

_____

_____

_____

How would it feel if your confident thoughts came true?

_____

_____

_____

Practicing the "What If?" Power Flip

(so you can master your emotions easier)

Negative "what if" questions:	How would you feel?
What if	
2)	
3)	

Now, do the POWER FLIP. Turn each negative question into a positive question.	How would you feel?
What if	
2)	
3)	

What could change if you forgive yourself?

_____

_____

_____

What if you decide to feel confident about your future?

_____

_____

_____

What if you feel confident that you can learn well?

_____

_____

_____

What if you choose to love and accept yourself no matter what?

_____

_____

_____

What if you decide to feel good about yourself?

_____

_____

_____

Now, make up some of your own positive questions and feel good!

_____

_____

_____

_____

_____

_____

_____

_____

Chapter 3
DOES IT WORK?

Chapter Goals

1. Know the "right" moves for taking charge

2. Use "school behavior" that works for you, not against you

3. Know how to get better responses from others

Getting Down to It

Do you use the same language with everyone? Do you behave the same way wherever you are? Do you just do what you feel like doing, whenever you want to?

Or do you use different words and actions for different situations?

Maybe you're just doing what you've always done because it feels comfortable. And it's true that no one can "make you" do or feel anything. In fact, the only person that can "make you" do anything is you! (But there might be a price to pay for not doing as asked.)

Take a moment to consider just how much control you really have. Do you know you have the power to analyze your options and choose your own future?

---

analyze – to figure out the parts of something or figure out how it works

confident, confidence – feeling sure

consider – think about

Fill In the Blanks

DIRECTIONS: Fill in the missing words below. Use words from the list below to fill in the blanks.

Does your _____ stay the same no matter where you <u>are</u>?
Do you _____ the same _____ with everyone you talk with?

Take a moment to consider just how much you really have. You have the _____ to analyze your _____ and _____ your own _____.

go   behavior   use   language   talking

consider   control   realize   power   options

future   choose

Take More Control of What You Do

As a teen, I doubted what most adults said. I thought I knew what was up. I was the master of the game. As far as I was concerned, adults were old-fashioned and unaware. All they wanted to do was

to keep me from having any fun. They were out of touch with my world. I didn't care what they had to say. Maybe you have felt that way?

It's true. Adults sometimes don't see what you have to deal with every day. They don't always listen or hear it right. Some grown people are out of touch with the

world of youth. However, whether adults see the point, hear the music, get a grip or not,

it's up to you to do whatever it takes to make your life count. Make your life work

FOR you and not against you. It's up to you to say the words that trigger the responses you're listening for.

Trigger Words

Have you ever had a conversation where you were misunderstood? The other person may have gotten angry at you. You instantly realized they just didn't get it. They completely misunderstood what you said. You knew by their response.

When someone hears something different from what we meant, we know it's time to adjust our delivery.

You may need to change your approach to get the responses you want. For example, what kind of responses do you want from your teachers—positive or negative?

Since you want responses that give you more freedom and make you feel good, complete the next activity and you'll truly understand.

Which Fits Best?

DIRECTIONS: For each place, list at least three behaviors that work. The first one has been done for you.

Rap concert	Park	Church	Court
scream			
dance			
listen			

School	The "streets"	Workplace	Home

Using behaviors that don't fit the situation is like walking on sharp rocks all day—OUCH!

What did you discover? How can you adapt your actions to fit the time, place, and people you're with?

_____

_____

_____

_____

Figure out exactly what you can do to improve your luck, solve your problems, and get people to respond the way you want them to. Will this benefit you right away?

Hmm...ya think?

Make the Right Moves to Take Charge

When someone doesn't respond the way you expect, maybe they just didn't get your true meaning. That means you need to say it differently. Keep changing your delivery until you get the desired response. That's called *adapting*.

I wish I had known that before!

People who adapt to fit the situation get more of what they want, AND they avoid needless trouble.

School-Appropriate Behavior

"School-appropriate" behavior is really "professional" behavior. It's the kind of behavior that gets adults off your back and gives you more control. We'll talk a little more about professional behavior in a minute, but first, list at least ten "school-appropriate" behaviors in the chart on the next page. We've listed a few for you:

Listen to your teacher.   Use your manners.

Follow your school's rules when using the internet.

Do your work.   No weapons.

Bring only useful materials to class.

Hang out with people who are on the road to success.

Now it's your turn. Write one school-appropriate behavior in each box below. You can use some from the list above.

agility – the ability to move quickly or figure things out quickly

adapt – change to fit the situation

Agility Is...?

Look at the picture below. What does "physical agility" mean? _____

_____

_____

What is an "agility challenge"? _____

_____

_____

What does it mean if someone has physical agility? _____

_____

_____

How about emotional agility? _____

_____

_____

Personal vs. Professional Life

From the time you were born, you've had a personal life. Everyone has a personal life. The dictionary defines "personal" as individual, private, special, or delicate. "Personal" refers to what we do when we're not at work or school. Examples are hobbies, sleeping, bathing (hopefully), and so on.

From the time you're old enough to enter school, you take on a professional life. Your profession is what you do for a living.

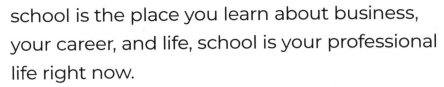

Why do people work or own a business? Some people work because they enjoy what they do. But everyone works for some type of pay. Since school is the place you learn about business, your career, and life, school is your professional life right now.

DIRECTIONS: Tell whether the behavior fits better into your personal life or your professional life. (Yes, some may fit in both).

Behavior	Personal or professional?
Clown around	both (when the teacher allows it at school)
Do work	
Play sports	
Sleep	
Work cooperatively with others	
Bathe or Shower	
Wear pajamas	
Use slang or "street language"	
Wear a swimsuit	
Negotiate (Use the "give to get" strategy)	
Use profanity	
Other:	
Other:	
Other:	

Although certain behaviors are appropriate in both your personal life and your professional life, watch out for anything in your personal life that keeps you from doing good business. Allowing your personal life to spill over into your professional life can cause many needless problems.

DIRECTIONS: Name two problems that can come from mixing your professional and personal life.

_____

_____

Ponder This

If you keep your personal and professional lives separate, you get to decide how to use your skills for each one.

How can you use this strategy to improve your life at home and at school (or work)?

Rate Your Skills: On a scale of 0 to 10, ten being strongest, how strong would you rate your ability to adapt right now? Circle a number.

0 1 2 3 4 5 6 7 8 9 10

How could you improve your ability to adapt?

_____

_____

VIDEO WATCH

We've all had a lot of unpleasant, unexpected events happen, especially over the last few years. It can feel upsetting.
This video gives you a way to handle it. Watch it now at:
https://youtu.be/2oDqaAuLDGQ

"How to Handle the Unexpected"

You can also go to YouTube
and search for EMOMASTERS or SELINAJOYJACKSON.

GAMEPLAY:

Games to empower you

Life Hacks and Music Love

Everyone in the world has been going through a lot during the pandemic.

The National Institute of Mental Health defines childhood trauma as "the experience of an event by a child that is emotionally painful or distressful, which often results in lasting mental and physical effects."

> **trauma** – a physical or psychological injury

However, difficulties – even tragedies – are a natural part of life. Learning how to cope (handle it) is important for your development.

- What if you could get over feeling stuck?
- What if you overcome the effects of trauma?
- What if you can feel safer and more in control over your life?

One way to do this is to use music to express your feelings. Musicians, singers, and songwriters do it all the time. There is amazing power in finding your voice and using it to uplift yourself and others.

Let's explore that!

Find music everywhere!

This music game is designed to help you make music. Check out one of Ms. Jackson's musical creations she made to help herself and others overcome negative effects when something bad happens. Then, come back and discover how to create your own.

VIDEO WATCH

Trauma Crossovers

https://www.youtube.com/watch?v=oUT21xHsRso

You can also go to YouTube

and search for EMOMASTERS or SELINAJOYJACKSON.

Songwriting 101

CHOOSE A SUBJECT:

1. Heartbreak
2. Power of words
3. Happily-ever-after love
4. Overcoming struggle
5. Choose your own

FROM LINES TO LYRICS

First Line Ideas:

- Ask a friend to give you the first line about your subject and go from there.
- Pick an emotion and write from there.
- Stop and look around you. Pick an object in your room and compare your subject to it.

MOVIE SCENES

Imagine you're writing this song for a TV show or movie. What is the setting? Where would it take place? A school? In your neighborhood? The city? An amusement park? Who is there?

Write about what you see.

Just let your words come to you.

Don't try to correct anything yet. This is the freestyle stage of songwriting.

RESOURCES

When you start to write lyrics, here are some resources to help you get into the flow:

- Rhyming dictionary – plenty of rhyming dictionaries are online, too. (Rhyming is fun, but lyrics don't have to rhyme.)
- Common idioms https://www.theidioms.com/. (An idiom [pronounced "IDD-ee-um"] is a saying whose meaning has become widely accepted.)

- What if you create your own Songwriter's Journal to keep your notes and lyrics?

What would a chicken sing about?

_____

_____

What would your friend sing about?

_____

_____

What would you sing about?

_____

_____

_____

_____

Now try writing some lyrics or just some topics for songs:

_____

_____

_____

_____

_____

_____

_____

_____

_____

_____

_____

_____

_____

_____

_____

_____

_____

Chapter 4
AUTHORITY RULES

Chapter Goals

1. Deal with authority figures in a way that benefits you

2. Give to Get—use negotiation skills to your advantage

3. Everything costs. What are you willing to pay?

Getting Down to It

At every level in society, there are authority figures: parents, guardians, the boss, law enforcement, the IRS, and so on.

Those who don't cooperate will find themselves dealing with them even more. There will always be someone who has the power to give you orders. Prisons are stacked with people who never understood this concept.

> **Power Play**
>
> To get someone to say "yes" more often, find out what that person wants and give it to them (if doing so keeps you SAFE and HEALTHY).

> **negotiate** – to discuss an agreement so both sides are satisfied

DIRECTIONS: Imagine being the one who makes the ultimate decision at school regarding consequences for bad behavior. What is a fair and effective (it works) consequence for each of the following behaviors?

Fighting -

Bullying -

Stealing -

Possessing a weapon -

Ditching class -

Possessing drugs -

Sexual harassment -

Using profanity -

Refusing to follow directions -

Not bringing books and materials to class -

Restricted Access

What is "permission"? How do you know when you have it? What kinds of things do you see, hear, or feel that let you know that you have freedom?

The opposite of "permission" is "restriction." Have you ever been grounded or put on restriction at home? If so, what was it like for you? Did you lose privileges?

I remember being grounded when I was

about sixteen. In our house, it was called "being in the dog-house." My foster mom came home from work one day and found the house empty. It was about 7:00 pm, and she instantly noticed something was wrong.

Shoes, jackets, and video games were strewn across the living room. The bedroom wasn't much better. Clothing was carelessly tossed on the bed and the closet floor. The kitchen was a disaster. The sink was overflowing with dirty dishes. Dirty pots and pans littered the stove. While leftover food sat on the table, we (my brother, sister, and I) were outside, down the street, hangin' out at the homies' crib. You know how it is.

The problem was that we hadn't completed our chores, so we got busted big time. I will never forget that one. I couldn't leave the house or talk on the phone for a month. I couldn't even watch TV! I hated not having permission.

Do you like having your freedom? Do you like your freedom enough that you are willing to do anything to protect it? Why is it important to protect your freedom?

_____

_____

_____

Why Use Your Freedom Wisely?

How do you define freedom? Does it mean you can do whatever you want and no one stops you, or does it mean no matter what happens, you ALWAYS have a choice? If you chose the first one, you need to know that definition doesn't have any "guardrails." What are guardrails? Why are guardrails important? Well, suppose someone wants your cell

phone and decides to just take it. When you ask for it back, they say, "No, I can keep it because I have the freedom to do anything I want." Is that really freedom? Nope.

Freedom means:

No matter what happens,

you ALWAYS have a choice.

Would you ride a rollercoaster that had no guardrails? Probably not. Those guardrails were put there to protect you because you are a valuable and worthwhile person. Certain rules and boundaries are in place to keep you safe.

What if you use your power of choice (your freedom) to make a positive difference for yourself? You could choose to make the best of any situation, and you could choose to find and focus on the good things in life.

Wait, what? You mean when something bad happens, there is something good happening, too? How does that work?

It's because some things in life are like that: you can't have a left without a right; you can't have an up without a down. When something bad happens in your life, there is a good side, even if it's small. The key is to focus on the good.

- What if you decide to focus on the good from now on?
- What if you let go of the fear of being overwhelmed?
- What if you allow yourself to feel confident and positive?
- What if you realize you always have a choice?

That's where your true power is!

Express Yourself

Many movies are about people who went through something bad but learned valuable lessons from it. Have you ever seen a movie like that? Tell about it:

Name of the movie:

_____

List some details describing how the person went through something bad and learned lessons from it.

_____

_____

_____

 Your freedom works best when you use it wisely. You don't cause needless trouble for anyone. Whenever you use your freedom wisely, you feel good about yourself. The bonus: you protect your freedom, too.

Skaters and Riders Show You How

If you ride a bike or skateboard, you probably know it's all about precision and accuracy. Jumping a skateboard successfully requires accuracy, timing, and fast reflexes.

If you go too slowly, you won't make the jump. If you go too fast, you could lose your balance or overdo the jump and land on your...

 On the other hand, it's amazing to see the riders who do it with skill and precision. They fly past each other at bone-breaking speeds, missing collisions by a hair. They slant on their boards at just the right angle to make those turns. It's geometry and physics in action. Expert riders do the math accurately.

Riders who miscalculate have bandages and casts instead of medals and trophies. They sit on the sidelines watching others have all the fun because strains, sprains, scrapes, and fractures take time to heal.

Those who plan their jumps ahead of time are more likely to make them successfully. Do you rush into situations without considering the possible consequences of your actions? If so, allow skateboards (and other things) to show you the lessons that work for you.

What does "jumping boards" show you about life?

_____

_____

_____

While reading this section, what did you discover about choices and consequences?

_____

_____

_____

What changes can you now make in your behavior to preserve your freedom easier and more enjoyably? (Check all that apply):

- ○ a. cooperate with the rules at school
- ○ b. avoid hanging out with troublemakers
- ○ c. do what pleases my parents
- ○ d. get involved in some positive hobbies or sports
- ○ e. find a positive and successful mentor (someone who has already done it and who will guide you)

Now, name two other things you can do to ensure that you KEEP your freedom:

_____

_____

With freedom comes responsibility.

--Eleanor Roosevelt

Standard Operating Procedures

When I was teaching in alternative education (for kids who get kicked out of regular school), the morning standard operating procedure (SOP) in my class was:

1. Come into class.

2. Sign in.

3. Turn in all electronic devices such as music players, cell phones, etc.

4. Get all necessary school supplies ready such as folders, pencils, etc.

5. Work on the assignment posted on the board.

6. When prompted, stand, push your chair in, and recite our class pledge.

You can see that the students who know what is expected are more successful and avoid a lot of problems. We had an SOP (Standard Operating Procedure) for the end of the day, too:

1. Put completed work in the black tray.

2. Put all class materials back where they belong.

3. Clean up any trash in your area.

4. When prompted, stand and deliver our closing statement.

5. Leave the campus immediately when dismissed.

SOPs are slightly different from class rules. Examples of rules:

- Complete all assignments accurately.
- Follow the teacher's directions.
- Keep hands, feet, and objects to yourself.

Rules are usually in place for safety, while SOPs are mostly for efficiency and effectiveness.

> **efficiency** – doing things the best way with the least waste of time and effort

Rules are usually consistent (or they're supposed to be) and are followed for the whole day.

SOPs depend on where you are and what you're doing, and they may be different for each class.

You've just discovered why you follow rules, and now you understand their purpose. Understanding how something works is empowering!

What is the purpose of rules? _____

_____

If you're unsure or there isn't an SOP, this could cause major problems for you, so ASK THE TEACHER.

DIRECTIONS: 1. Choose one of your classes. 2. List the SOPs for entering the room. 3. List the rules for the class.

Sample SOPs:	Sample Rules:
Enter the classroom quietly.	Keep hands and feet to yourself.
Put competed work in the blue tray.	No running in the classroom.

SOPs	Rules
1.	1.
2.	2.
3.	3.
4.	4.
5.	5.

Now list two benefits of cooperating with the rules and SOPs in your class or school:

_____

_____

If you are reading this book, you probably go to school. If you go to school, there's probably an SOP in each of your classes (or there should be). An SOP is:

- An organization's **required** way of doing things.

- **Necessary** to avoid chaos.

- **Important** so we can achieve exactly what we want to achieve easier.

Two problems you can avoid by following your school's SOP and rules are:

_____

_____

Sometimes life throws us a curve ball and we feel like we have no choices. The pandemic gave us reasons to feel trapped— as if we couldn't survive. It was difficult for billions of people. You're reading this book now, which shows you

have the power to overcome obstacles. You've already done so countless times. And despite the pandemic, you're still here. The key to overcoming obstacles, no matter how difficult they may feel, is to upgrade your mindset.

> What if you choose to agree to your classroom's SOPs and rules?
>
> Would you enjoy your school success when and how you choose? YES!

GAMEPLAY

A game to empower you to feel happier and freer

Infinity Hands

Put a piece of paper on your desk or table. Put a weight at the top of the sheet to hold it down so it doesn't move. Take two pencils or pens. Hold one in each hand. Now, draw an infinity symbol with each hand. It looks like a horizontal version of the number 8. Draw the symbols at the same time and don't stop or lift the pencils or pens for 60 seconds. This exercise helps you connect to both sides of your brain and expand your flexibility and creativity, which can help you solve problems easier. Isn't that good news? Now, go for it! Feel free to repeat this game a few times a week or when you want to solve a problem faster and easier.

Video Watch

Watch illustrator and graphic designer Jackie H., who created the characters in this book. She shares her first time using the infinity exercise to expand her creativity so she can be more successful and happier. See: Brain Boosting Magic: How to Do Crazy 8's: https://www.youtube.com/watch?v=exTYYJF-zLg

---

You can also go to YouTube and search for EMOMASTERS or SELINAJOYJACKSON.

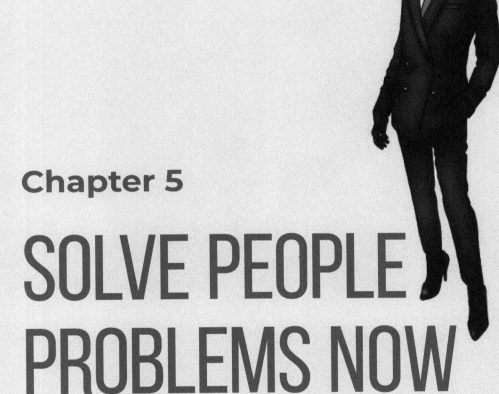

Chapter 5

SOLVE PEOPLE PROBLEMS NOW

Chapter Goals

1. Discover rapid solutions to people problems

2. See how to get others to say "yes" when they would usually say "no"

3. Learn how to deal with difficult people effectively

Getting Down to It

Do your folks yell at you too often? Do you get blamed for stuff you didn't do? Are you tired of teachers nagging at you to do better? Here is Robert's story:

Robert and I were having a conversation about a teacher he had been having trouble with.

He said, "Mr. Jones always yells at me. I don't like it, so I just won't do my work."

I asked, "So, you're saying that when the teacher yells, you respond by not doing your work?"

Robert answered, "Yeah, Ms. Jackson. If Mr. Jones wouldn't yell at me, I would do all my work."

I looked at him for a moment and replied, "Do you want to graduate?"

He looked at me as if I were crazy. "Of course. Come on, Ms. Jackson. What do you think, I'm stupid?"

I gazed at him for a moment and asked, "Well, if you don't do your work, will you graduate?"

He looked down and sighed out the answer. "No."

"If you don't do your work, who is really getting punished?"

"OK, OK, I get it." He got up with a knowing smile and went back to his classroom.

Sometimes we decide to change what we do.

Changing can let you keep control of your life, instead of giving control to someone else.

What could remind you to change to stay in control of your life? Draw a picture of it here.

Who Is Really Getting Punished?

DIRECTIONS: Answer the questions with <u>your</u> answers, not the answers you think adults want.

1. The teacher yells at you in front of the whole class. What's the first thing you usually say to yourself?

_____

_____

2. How do you feel when the teacher yells at you?

_____

_____

3. How do you usually respond if the teacher yells at you?

_____

_____

4. What do you want to happen when you respond that way (as in #3)?

_____

_____

5. Does it work without causing you even more problems?   Yes ___ No ___.

6. List other possible effects of yelling, cussing, or refusing to do your work:

Examples:

> *You get sent to the office.*

> *You miss class and fall behind.*

> *Your folks get called.*

> *You get detention or Saturday school.*

_____

_____

_____

7. What could it cost you? (Circle those that apply)

      time   respect   money   good grades

          reputation   privileges

8. What else could it cost you?

_____

_____

9. If someone does something you don't like, you get better results if you respond in a way that respects them and yourself. Name two ways to do that.

_____

_____

_____

Ponder this:

You are now older than when you first started school. You're growing up. That means you now have the maturity to respond in way that's respectful to yourself and to others.

Draw a picture of yourself responding in a way
that respects the other person and yourself.

10. What are some words you would use in your response?

_____   _____   _____   _____

_____   _____   _____   _____

Be curious!

I want you to be curious about something. If you yell, cuss, refuse to do your work, or throw tantrums when the teacher does something you don't like, who really gets punished?

I understand that teacher may have stepped out of line when they yelled at you. I also see how you might feel like getting back at them. And I don't blame you for feeling that way. When the teacher or any other adult does something you don't like, you can respond ANY WAY YOU CHOOSE. You can yell, cuss, refuse to follow directions, or not do your work.

But... at what cost?

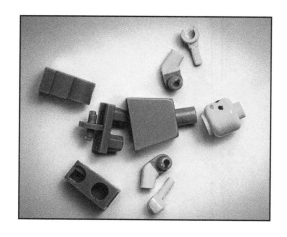

How to Get Teachers to Say "Yes" More Often

In a perfect world, all students would like all teachers and vice-versa, but we don't live in a perfect world, so:

1. How do you know when a teacher doesn't like you? List three things teachers might do when they don't like you:

   _____

   _____

   _____

2. When a teacher likes you, what problems do you avoid?

   _____

   _____

   _____

3. Akito is dealing with a teacher who does not like having him in class. Akito doesn't realize that he, too, has done some things that made the problem worse. List three things Akito may have done to get on the teacher's bad side.

   a. _____

   b. _____

   c. _____

4. What could Akito do to make the situation better?

DIRECTIONS: Check all that apply.

    a. Be quiet while others are working. ___

    b. Deal with disagreements in private. ___

    c. Avoid arguing with the teacher during class. ___

    d. Negotiate to get what he wants. ___

    e. Avoid bullying to get what he wants. ___

    f. Use professional language. ___

    g. Breathe deeply and talk calmly. ___

    h. Keep questions and comments on topic. ___

    i. Keep things calm for himself and others. ___

    j. Turn in his completed work on time. ___

    k. Always speak and act calmly. ___

    l. Avoid doing anything that could make it harder for teachers to do their jobs. ___

5. What does Akito's situation show you about:

Relationships: _____

Life: _____

6. Is it possible that Akito may want something from this teacher in the future? Check off one or more of the things he may want.

___ A "good news" letter

___ Free time

___ Fun activities

___ Good grades

___ A green light to his requests

During a conference with his teacher, she tells him, "When teachers get what *they* want, it's easier for you to get what *you* want." Akito decides to change his behavior.

Imagine Changing Your Life

1. Imagine you are doing very well in school. Draw a picture of yourself doing well in school.

2. When you're doing well in school, what do you hear the teacher and other adults saying to you? What are you saying to yourself?

_____

_____

_____

_____

_____

_____

3. Imagine doing extremely well in school. What does that feel like?

_____

_____

_____

Ms. Jackson says:

"As long as there are people, there will be people problems, but now <u>you</u> have the skills and the power to save yourself from unnecessary hassles."

It feels wonderful to have fewer "people problems," doesn't it?

Sometimes people problems happen just because you're young. Adults may not listen to you or value your opinion just because they are older. They mistakenly think that what you say doesn't count because you're younger. But, the truth is, what you have to say <u>is</u> important,

especially when it involves you and your life. Never let anyone devalue you just because you're young.

Listen Deeply

You used to have reasons to irritate your parents and teachers, but that's no longer useful. You can work with helpful adults in ways that satisfy you. And then you get to choose and enjoy the results!

GAMEPLAY

Games to empower you to feel happier and free

Ball Toss Mood Shifters

Grab a ball. As you toss or bounce it, ask yourself these positive "what if" questions to help shift your mood:

- What if this feeling is temporary?

- What if I can handle this?

- What if a wonderful, healthy idea comes to me that makes everything better?

- What if I ignore bad things and focus on good things?

You can choose to focus on what would happen if the problem were solved and you were feeling better.

How does this work?

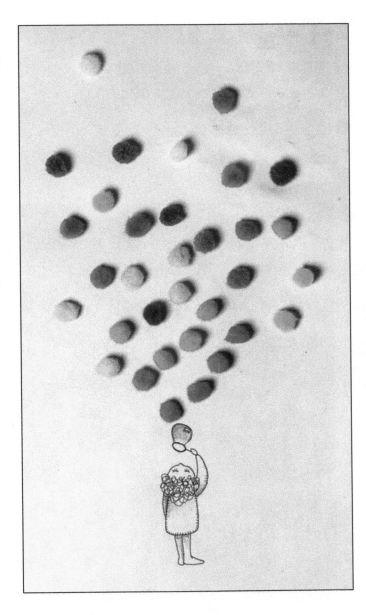

Anytime you're feeling an emotion, at least three things are involved:

1) Your body,

2) Your self-talk, and

3) What you're thinking about.

When you change one of those, your emotion changes. Changing all three is the most powerful.

The Ball Toss Mood Shifter gameplay above has you change all three!

Chapter 6
STREET LAW

Chapter Goals

1. Find and remove barriers to your success
2. Discover the secret codes for success
3. Get "them" off your back

Getting Down to It

My nieces and nephews came to visit one weekend. On Saturday afternoon, one of the girls told me someone had taken her candy.

I called a meeting where I explained that some candy had been taken. Immediately, her brother admitted he had eaten it. I thanked him for his honesty and then explained to them about the "safety code."

The "safety code" means every human deserves to be safe. You are human, so you deserve to be safe. Every human is valuable, worthwhile, and important. You are human, so you are valuable, worthwhile, and important.

Why do you think we have laws to protect you? Because you are valuable and so you can be safe. Believe that. You deserve it.

I told my nieces and nephews I understand they have to deal with a lot at school, and maybe even at home. I then asked, "Where do you feel safe?" One nephew shared that most of the time, he didn't feel safe at home. "Dang," I responded. "That's messed up." I shook my head.

"Well, everyone needs a place to feel safe. My home is a safe zone," I said. "It is ruled by the safety code. Therefore, there's no need to worry about whether you or your belongings will be harmed. Making fun of each other, giving each other a bad time, and any other kind of abuse is off limits. Instead, you can spend time here doing more of the things you enjoy. If you violate this code, you lose your space here. Make sense?"

We all agreed and spent the weekend drawing, painting, and playing basketball, tennis, and video games. We went to the movies and belly-laughed. We ate pizza, hamburgers, salad, and fruit. Cookies, chips, and candy were available, too. It was heaven. And since I've had enough of the other place, heaven works for me. How about you?

Name three places you can go when you want to relax and feel worry-free:

_____

_____

_____

Success Rules

What is a rule? What is a code? That's just two names for the same thing. Rules and codes are directions that tell you what you can and cannot do in certain situations. What is their purpose? Rules and codes are to help you stay safe and be successful. Just as there are rules for different types of games, there are rules for different places.

Name three rules of your favorite sport:

_____

_____

_____

What is the purpose of having rules in sports?

_____

_____

_____

Sometimes exceptions to rules can be made. Other times there are no exceptions. That's when you may feel frustrated, let-down, or mad, especially if in the past you've been allowed to get around it or "slide." Sometimes, well-meaning people believe they're helping you by letting you get around the rules. But that's not how it usually is in the real world. In the real world, you have to cooperate with rules to get what you want.

Do You Know the Code?

One important hidden code of success in school is to avoid laughing when an adult is talking to you about a problem. Laughing when an adult is in "correction mode" spoils your success and brings even more trouble breathing down your neck. Instead, keep a straight face and look like you're sorry, even if you don't feel that way. Sometimes you just gotta play the game.

But I don't wanna play the game!

Another school success rule is: Education can give you the power to climb the success ladder and make good money. Even though you might not think it's necessary or do-able, it's important to take your education seriously and use it to improve your life.

Secret Codes of Success

Most places have known rules, but many places have some secret codes of behavior that aren't known by everyone.

Knowing these hidden rules can help you be successful where you are.

If you don't know them, you'll have problems.

Now, let's discover some other secrets that have been causing some people a lot of problems.

When I was teaching in alternative education, some of my students hung out in the streets or knew people from the streets. What are some of the hidden rules on the streets? "Never let 'em see you sweat," "Don't show fear or weakness," "Don't trust anybody," and so on.

DIRECTIONS: Name two more.

1. _____

2. _____

These "street laws" dictate how people think and act on the streets. If you don't know them, then you just get caught slippin'. But if you use this same set of rules at work or school, what could happen?

Complete the next exercise and you'll have more control over what happens to you. Now, who doesn't want that?

DIRECTIONS: Write "school rules," "street law," or "both" in the blanks. The first one has been done for you.

I want it; I take it.	*street law*
I use my language to negotiate.	
I'll get them before they get me.	
I am willing to work for what I want.	
I make good choices now for a better future.	
I use my language to intimidate	
I have to prove how tough I am.	
Education and achievement are important to me.	
I do what needs to be done, whether I feel like it or not.	
I must protect my "tough guy" reputation.	
I use non-aggressive ways to protect myself.	
When someone does something I don't like, I respond in ways that are respectful to myself and to others.	
It's OK to take the law into my own hands.	
I handle anger in ways that create even more problems.	
I use aggression or intimidation to get what I want.	

I use words to embarrass people.	
I find healthy ways to express my feelings.	
I get your permission before I touch your belongings.	
Adults are here to protect me.	
I keep a straight face and avoid laughing when I or someone else is being disciplined.	

"La Vida Loca"

How do you feel when someone takes something of yours without your permission? Do you feel offended? Do you feel like it's unsafe for you to leave your belongings sitting around? Do you feel suspicion? Taking something without permission is a "street element." Taking the law into your own hands, using force, or bullying to get your way is how it's done in the streets.

Revenge

Sometimes people say things we don't like. They may do things we consider rude or mean. When this happens, revenge may be

tempting. When someone does something you don't like, how do you usually respond?

_____

_____

_____

_____

We are not living in a movie

1. Name a movie where one or more characters use violence or take revenge on another character. Briefly tell how the character takes revenge.

_____

_____

_____

_____

2. What are some consequences of bringing "street law" into the classroom?

_____

_____

_____

_____

3. Your physical and emotional safety will be threatened if schools allow what?

_____

_____

_____

_____

4. What is the difference between "ratting someone out" (also called snitching) and "informing for safety"?

_____

_____

_____

_____

_____

_____

5. Some describe "cussing" as the language of shock and survival. Explain.

_____

_____

_____

6. Fighting may give some status and protection on the streets, but not anywhere else. Explain how fighting can cause even more problems.

_____

_____

_____

7. What does "self-defeating" mean?

_____

_____

_____

8. How is street behavior self-defeating?

_____

_____

_____

_____

9. Your safety begins with you. Why or why not?

_____

_____

_____

_____

10. Pretend someone does something that your friend doesn't like. Tell how your friend would usually respond.

_____

_____

_____

_____

11. What are some possible consequences of using "street talk" in school?

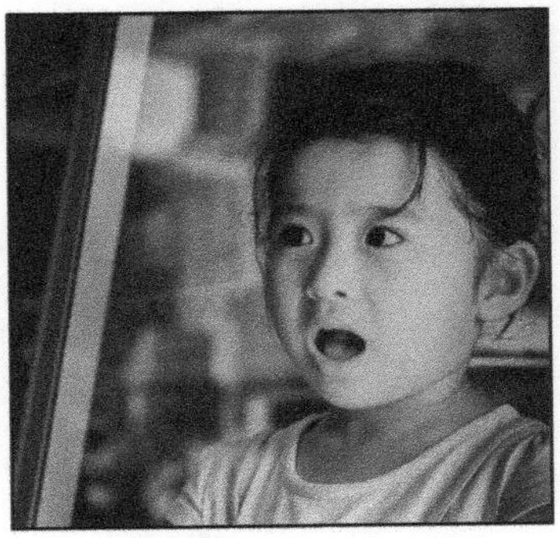

_____

_____

_____

12. Suppose you were teaching your little brother or sister how to use "professional language." Which of the phrases below are most meaningful to you? (Choose at least three and underline your choices.)

I feel...   The problem is...   I prefer...   I want...

I am aware of...   What I meant to say is...   I don't like...

I am not willing to...   I feel annoyed about...

I would rather...   Can we talk about this later?

I feel comfortable with...   I feel uncomfortable with...

13. What are some "professional" words you could use when you tell someone you don't like what they did?

_____

_____

_____

_____

14. Draw a picture of yourself using "professional language" successfully.

15. Name at least three benefits of using "professional language" where it fits.

_____

_____

_____

_____

16. We all need a place where we can go and be safe. A safe zone is where you can relax, enjoy, and just "be." Home is supposed to be that place. Do what you can to make it that way. School is the next best place. What can you do to make school a safe zone now?

_____

_____

_____

_____

Do It Like the PROs

If you get angry at school the way some people do in the streets, it will cause big problems for you and your loved ones.

So, you need to find ways to express strong emotions,

but in a professional way.

Why? Because school is

your "professional" life right now.

What you do in your spare time is your "personal" life and

what you do at school is your "professional" life.

You need to know the difference between them and keep them separate.

People who don't know this lose far more than they ever expected.

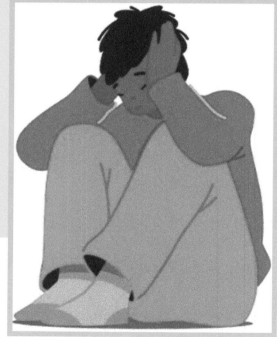

GAMEPLAY

Real life has rules. The rules exist to protect you so you can have a long, healthy, and happy life. The rules for driving are to protect you, too.

These important road signs help keep you safe on the road. You can also think of them as advice for life.

Choose three. What advice does each one give you about your life?

Your Sign Choice	Your Personal Life Message

LIFE LESSON:

School is the place for you to practice cooperating now.

It will make your future success easier,

and you'll avoid a lot of problems.

Chapter 7
GET THE RESPECT YOU DESERVE

Chapter Goals

1. Get respect from your peers without fighting
2. Defuse hotheads faster and easier
3. Increase your safety, success, and well-being

Getting Down to It

Do you want powerful ways to make your school safer?

Do you want to achieve YOUR goals more easily? Do you want to avoid needless trouble? Why is this important?

With more and more school violence, you may be thinking, "Why bother?" But you may also be thinking how wonderful it would be to feel calm at school. Let's see what we can do.

Leave the drama on TV, where it belongs.

Express Yourself

In this section, we will expose some secrets that cause problems for a lot of people. Let's get started!

1. How would you define **fear**?

_____

2. How would you define **respect**?

_____

3. Which would you prefer in school: to be feared or respected? Why?

_____

_____

_____

Compare the two words FEAR and RESPECT in the Venn diagram:

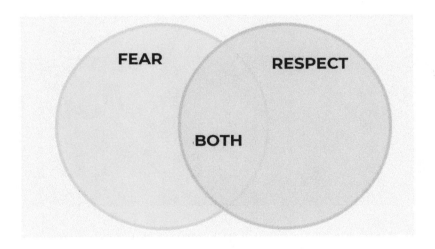

They overlap! What does that mean for you?

_____

_____

_____

_____

_____

Hide-and-Seek

Most of us have played Hide-and-Seek. Part of the fun in this game is finding ways to out-smart or out-run the person who is trying to get us. When we make it to the base before being tagged out, we say we're "safe."

1. How physically safe do you feel at school? Circle a number.

   1   2   3   4   5   6   7   8   9   10

   Not Safe   Very Safe

2. How emotionally safe do you feel at school? Circle a number.

   1   2   3   4   5   6   7   8   9   10

   Not Safe   Very Safe

DIRECTIONS: Check those that are important to you.

___ To feel safe	___ Friends
___ Respect	___ Fun
___ Love	___ Excitement
___ Freedom	___ Variety (no boredom)
___ Attention	___ To feel understood
___ To feel capable	___ To fit in
___ To feel happy	___ To feel important
___ To be appreciated	___ Good grades

SAFE ZONE

Making your school a safe place is partly up to you. What could happen if you don't? Here's what could happen:

You or someone you love could get hurt.

You or someone you love could get expelled.

You or someone you love could lose their freedom.

You or someone you love could die.

Violence, the Hard Way

Is it easier to do what you want when you feel safe? I will now "break the rules" and treat you like the mature, smart, understanding person you are. Serious "grown-up" stuff: Has it occurred to you that when you feel unsafe, you spend a lot of time watching your back—time you could use to do what you want to do?

Nothing is as distracting as the feeling that someone is "out to get you." It takes your attention from all the interesting and fun things happening around you. It can put you into painful situations.

DIRECTIONS: Answer the questions below.

1. Who do you know who has lost family members, friends, or classmates to violence?

_____

_____

_____

2. How were they affected?

_____

_____

_____

3. Is this something you want to deal with? _____

4. What kinds of things would you prefer to deal with instead?

_____

_____

_____

The Fight

"Oo-oo-oh, that was a good fight this morning. Did you see it?

"Yeah, somebody told her that the girl was talking about her mom, and she ran up and asked her if it was true. The girl started talkin' a bunch of stuff and told her to 'come on,' and then swung on her..."

"Uh, huh, and then she swung back... and they started fightin'. I thought she was gonna win the way she ran up on that girl, but she..."

"She got messed up! Bet she didn't know she was gonna catch a beat-down from that girl."

"Too bad the teacher had to break it up. I wanted to see some more action."

"Did they get suspended?"

"I heard she's getting expelled after she gets out of the hospital."

"Then I know that girl is gonna get expelled, too. After they took her to the hospital, the police rolled up, hand-cuffed the other girl, and took her to jail. They're charging her with assault."

"Can they DO that? I mean, it was just a little fight at school."

"I heard you could get arrested anytime you fight at school, especially if someone gets hurt."

"I'm glad it wasn't me. I mean, one person is hurt bad; the other is in jail. She didn't have to run up on that girl like that. I say she started it."

"I know... getting up in her face like she wanted to fight."

"But the other girl didn't have to start talkin' trash, either."

"Yeah, I know, but you have to admit... it was still *a good fight!*"

It's only good when you're in the ring and getting paid for it!

(I mean if boxing is what you really want to do: dodge swinging fists, hoping NOT to catch one... WAIT... What!?)

What Do You Think?

1. List some things someone could do to make sure a fight will start.

_____

_____

_____

_____

2. Why do students usually fight at school?

_____

_____

_____

_____

R U Chicken?

If you fight at school because you're trying to prove to others that you're not chicken, then you really are chicken, because you are afraid of what others think!

3. Why is fighting at school a bad way to protect yourself?

_____

_____

_____

"It's been six months, and I'm still trying to pull myself together!"

4. What are some better ways to protect yourself?

_____

_____

You are older than when you first started school. You are reading this now. Are you getting better at handling conflict at school and at home? If so, you can feel very good about yourself. Others will probably notice your efforts, too, even if they don't say anything.

Increase your power and self-confidence. Say the Power Play statements below aloud whenever you need this boost. You know best when to use them.

Power Play Statements

What if I could get along better with everyone? YES!

What if I could avoid trouble? YES!

What if I could feel happy and strong? YES!

What if I could make the right kind of friends? YES!

What if my success is in my hands? YES!

What if I could make better choices? YES!

Any questions?

GAMEPLAY

Games to empower you to feel happier and free

Tic-Tac-Toe Blackout Interview

Choose a family member, classmate, or friend. Ask them one of the questions below and pay attention to their responses. Then write their name in the box. Make sure you choose a different person for each box. This can help you strengthen your relationships. That's very helpful!

If you chose a hashtag to describe your life right now, what would it be? Name: _____	If you were to create a national holiday, what would it be? Name: _____	Who do you admire most and why? Name: _____
What is one hidden talent or strength you have that you wish people knew about? Name: _____	What do you think is the biggest danger when kids use the internet? Name: _____	If you started a band, what would you name it and why? Name: _____
When life is rough, what do you do to encourage yourself? Name: _____	What negative emotions do you sometimes feel when using Instagram, Tik-Tok, or _____? Name: _____	Who makes you smile most? Name: _____

VIDEO WATCH

When you have a conflict with someone, how do you stop your emotions from taking over? Find out here:

"Are You Being Controlled by an Emotional Takeover?"

https://www.youtube.com/watch?v=cE8i_dXF1JA&t=50s

You can also go to YouTube

and search for EMOMASTERS or SELINAJOYJACKSON.

Chapter 8
BULLY-PROOF YOURSELF

Chapter Goals

1. Discover the three secrets bullies don't want you to know

2. Become invisible to bullies and powerful to peers

3. Make wise decisions and avoid needless trouble

Getting Down to It

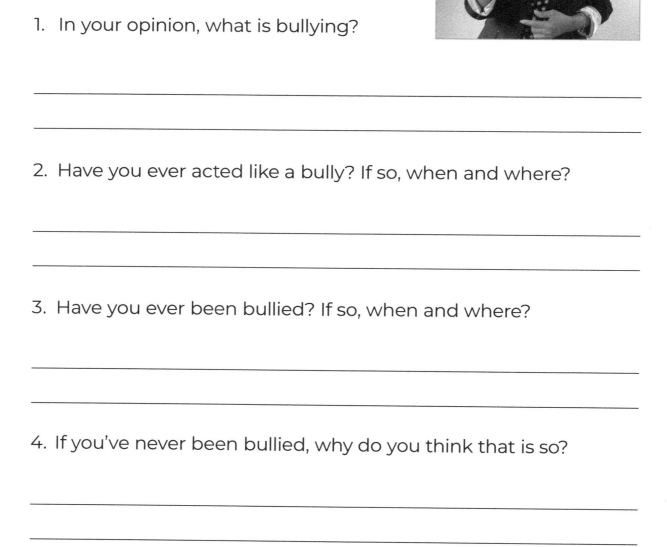

From the start, let me say: No one wants to look weak, look like a wimp, or lose status in their peer group. Read on to find out how you can avoid that.

1. In your opinion, what is bullying?

_____

_____

2. Have you ever acted like a bully? If so, when and where?

_____

_____

3. Have you ever been bullied? If so, when and where?

_____

_____

4. If you've never been bullied, why do you think that is so?

_____

_____

A lot of bullying that happens in schools is not reported, but the harmful results of bullying last a lifetime. That's important.

You can help keep your school safe. Then you can relax and pay more attention to achieving what you really want to do.

5. Use the information in the box above to fill in the missing words:

Studies show that a lot of _____ happens in _____ and is not _____. The harmful _____ of bullying can last a _____.

What is a Bullying Incident?

It's fun to joke around with your friends and classmates, tease, or horseplay. Usually, these are not considered bullying when they happen with certain people. But here's the difference:

- If a person uses their size, strength, or influence to scare someone (or get others to scare someone), that's bullying.

- If a person deliberately causes pain or worry, that's bullying.

- If the person does that over and over with the same people, that's bullying!

How do you know when a bullying incident is taking place?

_____

_____

_____

What do bullies hope to accomplish?

Bullies are looking for power. They might not feel powerful anywhere else in their lives. You could say that anyone who acts like a bully secretly feels powerless.

If I'm not getting bullied, why should I care?

The effects of bullying last a lifetime. It causes stress for victims and people who witness bullying. They are scarred for life, even if they don't know it. Also, if this cruelty isn't stopped, it will continue and will soon affect you or someone you care about. Bullying hurts everybody.

Are things BAD ENOUGH NOW to make a change, or do you want to wait until things are EVEN WORSE?

1. What do bullies hope to accomplish?

_____

_____

2. If you're not getting bullied, why should you care?

_____

_____

Don't bullies only hit their victims?

No. Four kinds of bullies exist, and they all affect your social life.

Physical	Verbal	Relational	Reactive
They hit or kick to intimidate or cause pain.	They use words to cause pain, harass, abuse, or scare people. This includes name-calling and repeated teasing.	They deliberately leave someone out (exclude them) and get others to reject them, too.	The bully provokes a person to react to the bully so the bully can fight back in "self-defense." (Not easily recognized)
Hits others to cause injury, scare them, or destroy their property.	Spreads ugly rumors about the victim, in person or online.	Usually combined with verbal abuse.	They make themselves look like the victim, then use that as an excuse to attack the victim.

verbal – using words

intimidate – to scare

harass – to deliberately bother somebody

provoke – to make somebody angry

relational – about relationships

Your Experience

DIRECTIONS: Describe an event from your own experience that fits one or more of the four categories of bullying.

_____

_____

_____

_____

_____

_____

_____

_____

_____

_____

_____

_____

_____

_____

What are some consequences that bullies can expect to have?

_____

_____

_____

If bullies don't stop bullying, things will get worse, and they will find themselves in HOT WATER! Here's what bullies can expect:

- People around them won't like them.

- They start to make enemies.

- Since most other people don't want to be around a bully, the bully starts to hang out with other bullies, or the bully joins a gang. Then they have to watch their backs even more.

- Their families start to suffer and could even be killed because of their actions.

- They usually have more addiction, substance abuse (alcohol, drugs, etc.), and mental health problems.

- Their relationships with loved ones go bad.

List at least three consequences bullies can expect:

_____

_____

_____

What if I allow myself to be a victim of a bully?

It's not your fault. I have worked with young people for over 30 years, and I have discovered that bullies look for power that's easy to get. They are always looking for people who are alone or who look like easy victims. They look for people who hold their heads down rather than standing tall; and people who shuffle, waddle, or drag themselves along. People who mumble or whine are targets, too.

But no matter how you walk or talk, being bullied is NEVER your fault. Bullies are responsible for their own actions.

What are the three secrets that bullies never want anyone to know? Turn the page to find out.

Secret #1	Secret #2	Secret #3
A bully needs an audience.	**Bullies cover up their fear by being mean.**	**Bullies depend on other people to help them feel good about themselves.**
They enjoy having people watch them in action. That makes them feel powerful.

If someone watching says, "Come on, let's get out of here," and then leaves, the bully loses power. | Bullies use their words and actions to convince others that they are "big and bad," when, actually, deep down inside, they are fearful.

Bullies try to force people to give them what they want.

It takes strength and courage to find better ways to get what you want. | They feel they are of little or no value, so they look to others to help them feel good about themselves.

But they don't know this, so they will deny it until they develop some maturity, which might never happen. |

DIRECTIONS: Mark the correct answers.

1. Which people do bullies look for?

    ☐ People who appear weak.

    ☐ People who hold their heads down or slouch rather than standing straight.

    ☐ People who mumble rather than speak up.

    ☐ People who are usually alone.

    ☐ People who shuffle, waddle, or drag along when they walk.

    ☐ People who speak in a squeaky or whiney voice.

> **Self-esteem** is self-respect.

Studies say bullies have low self-esteem, so if you were the most successful counselor in the world, what three things would you suggest a person could do to feel better about themselves? (Make sure they're things that work.)

_____

_____

_____

_____

_____

_____

Do you think about your sister or brother, or your friends, or your friends' brothers and sisters? What can you do so loved ones don't get bullied?

Research shows that bullying stops when it is reported and the bully gets serious consequences for their behavior. But some students don't want to report it because they don't want to be called a "snitch," "narc," or "rat."

confidential - secret

There's good news, though. You can report bullying incidents to teachers or other school staff privately. That means your peers don't have to know who reported the bullying.

Then, make sure the school follows through. It's the law!

1. What can students do to eliminate bullying?

_____

_____

2. Imagine a school with no bullies. What would it be like to go to a school like that?

_____

_____

_____

Bully-Proof: Test Your Skills

DIRECTIONS: Answer the questions based on what you just read. Mark the correct answers.

1. A verbal bully is one who:

    O a. Uses words to hurt, embarrass, or humiliate someone.

    O b. Uses sticks and stones to break your bones.

    O c. Uses the dictionary to look up synonyms for the word "bully."

2. A physical bully:

    O a. Performs difficult physical activities.

    O b. Excludes others.

    O c. Hits, kicks, or damages property.

3. A reactive bully:

    O a. Creates a situation in which they look as if they are the victim so they can fight back and then claim "self-defense."

    O b. Is often difficult to recognize.

    O c. All of the above.

4. If one of your classmates tells you (and others) not to be friends with someone, this is:

   O a. A reactive bully.

   O b. A relational bully.

   O c. A verbal bully.

5. All of the following are possible consequences that a bully can expect, EXCEPT:

   O a. They make enemies and their popularity goes down.

   O b. Their families get hurt and suffer.

   O c. They'll get out of jail free.

6. A bullying incident occurs when:

   O a. There is a power struggle between the victim and the bully.

   O b. The victim tries to hurt, embarrass, or humiliate the bully.

   O c. Intentional, cruel incidents happen over and over, with the same people in the same bully and victim roles.

7. Bullies hope to accomplish the following:

   O a. They want to achieve power.

   O b. Deep down, they want to feel good about themselves.

   O c. Both a and b.

8. Research shows that bullying STOPS when:

   O a. The bully is anonymous.

   O b. It is reported and action is taken.

   O c. None of the above.

9. When students don't feel safe, they are more likely to have:

   O a. Stress.

   O b. Headaches.

   O c. Other illnesses.

   O d. All of the above.

10. Bullying is:

    O a. Cruel.

    O b. Inhumane.

    O c. Emotionally damaging.

    O d. All of the above.

Fill-in-the-Blank

DIRECTIONS: Fill in the missing words below.

1. Bullies who socially exclude their victims are called _____ bullies.

2. Bullying is a series of repeated incidents involving the _____ people.

3. Bullying is considered _____ (against the law).

4. The effects of bullying last a _____ .

5. If you allow bullying to continue, it will continue until it affects _____.

6. Bullies usually have more alcoholism, drug abuse, and mental health _____.

7. Bullies use their behavior and words to try to convince others that they are "big and bad," but they actually feel _____.

8. Bullies thrive on having an audience _____ them in action.

9. Studies say bullies have low _____.

Safe schools:

- Are peaceful places

- Respect and care about all students and staff

- Encourage responsibility, confidence, and self-esteem

- Are supportive and healthy

- Encourage and appreciate diversity and differences

Draw a picture of a safe school:

When your school is safe, you can achieve success faster and more enjoyably! Draw at least three things you'd see in your school if it were safer:

Express Yourself

1. What needs to happen so you feel safe enough to let an adult know when bullying is happening?

_____

_____

2. Name three ways a person can report a bullying incident anonymously (in secret).

_____

_____

Pretend you are a parent. What would you tell your child to do to stop the bullying?

_____

_____

GAMEPLAY

MIRROR MAGIC

What Confident People Do

Often, people get picked on or don't get what they want because they appear to lack confidence. What if you could have powerful self-esteem and unstoppable confidence? You need to understand some secrets about communication.

Whenever you communicate, people pick up your nonverbal messages. That means how you say it is important. When talking with adults, if you yell or talk in a mean tone of voice, they get insulted or feel disrespected. Wouldn't you feel that way, too?

Your tone comes across in four nonverbal ways:

1. **Your eyes**: are they rolling, squinted tight, wide open, friendly, or threatening?

2. **Your voice**: Is it loud or soft? Fast or slow? High voice or low voice? Whether you're growling or speaking calmly, this changes how the listener understands your words.

3. **Your body** (posture): Do you look strong, stable, and grounded? Where are your arms? Is there a slouch in your back, or are you standing tall?

4. **Your breathing**: Is it shallow or deep? Is it a calm flow, or does it seem like a struggle?

Stand in front of the mirror

If you feel as if you have no control over your life, you can change that by boosting your confidence. This gameplay can help.

Pretend you are feeling unsure of yourself. How would your eyes look? Put your body language in that mode. How do people stand when they are feeling unsure of themselves? How about breathing? Now, say something like, "I don't feel very sure of myself." Make sure to sound unconfident for this part. Take note of your four nonverbals.

Now, what if, deep inside, you have unstoppable confidence? Stand that way. Use your body to show that.

What if you put that confident look in your eye? What changes? When you're feeling confident, what is your breathing like?

Now, use your most confident voice: Say, "I feel very confident that I can do it, or I can learn how!"

Take note of your four nonverbals. Shift back and forth a couple of times from feeling unsure to feeling confident. Notice the difference. Draw a picture of yourself feeling confident.

DIRECTIONS: Fill out the chart and compare the nonverbal communication you practiced a moment ago.

	What did you do with your eyes? To appear unsure: To appear confident:
	What differences did you notice in your body language? (Be careful, don't let crossed arms fool you. That doesn't necessarily mean confidence.) To appear unsure: To appear confident:
	Now, compare your breathing. Faster? Slower? Steady? To appear unsure: To appear confident:
	What did you do with the sound of your voice? To appear unsure: To appear confident:

VIDEO WATCH

"Free to Live Your Best Life"

Here's the link:
https://youtu.be/q-VaSpcvs0U

Is your definition of confidence working for
or against you?

"How Do You Define Confidence?"

https://youtube.com/shorts/iPWhwWAc_hU

You can find these videos on YouTube

by searching for EMOMASTERS or
SELINAJOYJACKSON.

You've learned a lot! Do you feel better about your future? Tell why
or why not:

_____

_____

_____

_____

_____

_____

A Few Words from Ms. Jackson

Has anyone asked you, "What do you want to be when you grow up?"

Has anyone asked you, "What *kind of person* do you want to be?"

Maybe someone has told you, "You can be whatever you want to be."

I'm here to tell you: You can be whatever *kind of person* you want to be.

When I was growing up, no one told me I could choose to be the kind of person people admire. I had to find out on my own. I discovered that I could choose to be successful, honest, confident, and have powerful self-esteem.

But before I learned that, I caused needless trouble for myself. For example, I was scared to say *no* to my friends when I didn't want to go along with something bad. I struggled for too long, so I lost things that were important to me—things like friendships with people who care.

Because I care, I'm sharing this with you so you can create your future success and happiness.

So: What kind of person do you want to be?

Selina Joy Jackson, M.A.

Post-Program Survey, Part 1

1. Hitting is the best way to protect myself. _____

2. Other people sometimes make me mad. _____

3. Sometimes at school, I have to be mean to get what I want. _____

4. My anger causes problems for me. _____

5. Good grades are important to me. _____

6. The teachers are responsible for my education. _____

7. Sometimes I have to cuss someone out. _____

8. I expect to be a college student someday. _____

9. I can control how I feel. _____

10. Other people decide what my future will be. _____

11. I worry about my safety in school. _____

12. Before I do anything, I usually think about what could happen. _____

13. If my friend does something bad, I keep it a secret. _____

14. I worry about what others will think if I avoid a fight at school. _____

15. Having fun is more important than learning. _____

16. I can change how I feel by changing how I think. _____

Continue to Part 2

Post-Program Survey, Part 2

DIRECTIONS: Answer the questions below in your own words.

1. Is it easy for you to pay attention to the teachers when you're at school? Why or why not?

2. How does your family influence your decisions?

3. What will you be doing one year from now?

4. What will you be doing five years from now?

About This Program

This program follows guidelines as established by:

- Title IV Safe and Drug Free Schools and Communities Act
- Safe Schools for Safe Learning Act (authorized by California Assembly Bill 514)
- Character Education (California Department of Education)

This program is based on practices found to be effective for violence-prevention programs, such as those mentioned above. This program provides school-age children with resources to help them cope effectively with the feelings, thoughts, and behaviors that frequently appear after traumatic events such as hurricanes, earthquakes, accidents, wildfires, pandemics, bullying, and other negative experiences. For people of any age, there may be no outwardly visible signs of injury, yet the emotional toll can be severe and life-limiting.

Although this workbook is designed to reach students ages 10 through 18 (critical developmental years), concepts and ideas in this book can be modified to use with any age group.

This workbook:

- Teaches violence-prevention skills through interactive methods such as:
  - modeling,
  - role-playing,
  - discussion,
  - group feedback,

- ○ reinforcement, and

- ○ extended practice;

- Fosters pro-social bonding to the school and community,

- Teaches social competence (communication, self-efficacy, assertiveness),

- Teaches culturally and developmentally appropriate social skills,

- Promotes positive peer influence,

- Emphasizes skills-training teaching methods,

- Uses periodic evaluation to determine the program's effectiveness,

- Uses conflict resolution and violence-prevention curricula,

- Introduces cooperative learning,

- Offers classroom behavior-management techniques, and

- Uses interrelated instructional strategies designed for continuous progress.

This program is also in harmony with the California Department of Education's guidance for Transformative Social and Emotional Learning (TSEL), which reflect the critical role of positive relationships and emotional connections in the learning process and help students develop a range of skills they need for school and life in general. These skills include the ability to:

- set and achieve positive goals,

- feel and show empathy for others,

- establish and maintain positive relationships,

- make responsible decisions, and

- understand and manage emotions.

It is the author's hope that this workbook will be used to improve the lives of children everywhere by giving them the social and emotional self-management skills needed to thrive in an often-difficult world. All children have tremendous potential. Let's show them how they can translate that potential into better lives.

COMMON CORE REFERENCE GUIDE FOR ENGLISH LANGUAGE ARTS/ ENGLISH LANGUAGE DEVELOPMENT FRAMEWORK

- Meaning Making
  - Making Meaning with Complex Text
- Language Development Vocabulary
- Effective Expression
  - Writing, Discussing, Presenting
- Content Knowledge – Engaging with Informational Text
- Foundational Skills
- Developing the readiness for college, careers, and civic life; Connecting learning to their future adult life, expanding cognitive abilities

Visual Arts Framework

- Use senses to perceive works of art, objects in nature, events, and the environment
- Create original artworks based on personal experiences or responses
- Derive meaning from artworks through analysis, interpretation, and judgment

Bloom's Taxonomy

1. Knowledge - define, identify, list, match, name, recall, tell, state
2. Comprehension - convert, describe, explain, interpret, restate, retell, summarize, translate
3. Application - apply, conclude, demonstrate, draw, illustrate, state a rule or principle
4. Analysis - analyze, compare, contrast
5. Synthesis - change, compose, create, suggest, visualize, write
6. Evaluation - Choose, compare, conclude, decide, give an opinion

Multiculturalism

- Integrate appreciation of cultural diversity into all class activities
- Allow student engagement in appreciation of cultural strengths of all groups
- Teach learners how they learn
- Develop rapport with students

Search Institute's Asset Development

Students experience the following developmental assets as they participate in the EMOMASTERS™ activities.

External Assets	Internal Assets
Support	Commitment to learning
Empowerment	Positive values
Boundaries and expectations	Social competencies
Constructive use of time	Positive identity

Ingredients for successful group programs include:

1. Developing trust and support by:
   - protecting everyone's right to express opinions without being attacked,
   - recognizing strong and positive individuals in the group and use them as leaders of small groups.
2. Promoting student responsibility by:
   - turning questions and problems back to the group,
   - letting them answer and discuss alternatives to problems that may arise.
3. Focus on success by
   - reinforcing appropriate behavior, no matter how minor,
   - using failure as a learning experience.

Index